Naiem ahmadinejadfarsangi

Mohammad Hossein Yusuf Elahi

Naiem ahmadinejadfarsangi

Mohammad Hossein Yusuf Elahi

Al-Okrah Literary Festival winner

Noor Publishing

Publisher:
Noor Publishing
is a trademark of
Dodo Books Indian Ocean Ltd., member of the OmniScriptum S.R.L Publishing group
str. A.Russo 15, of. 61, Chisinau-2068, Republic of Moldova Europe
Printed at: see last page
ISBN: 978-620-4-72300-6

Mohammad Hossein Yusuf Elahi

Naiem ahmadinejadfarsangi

Table of Contents

It rains, the soil calls you in its frequent breaths and praises your greatness.

The trees have fixed their eastern eyes on your sun and are standing in praise of your holy lights.

God! Creation worships your divine presence day and night, and the particles of existence call you lovingly. Or Rahman or Rahim! I need your dignity and forgiveness. Help me to remove the rust of sin and ugliness from my heavy heart.

Forgive me and forgive me, so that I may learn to fly, the restless bird of my soul, in the sky of your kindness.

Help me to turn to your friendship in this deserted desert.

O Eternal Endless! Your seekers are the residents of the alleys of knowledge and thought; They only hear and see you every moment of their lives; mystics whose eternal abode is the pavilions of your love; God! Make me their neighbor so that the blind side of the light of their eyes will sit in my eyes and the dark world of my heart will hope for the arrival of a bright day.

God! My lips are thirsty for your mercy and my soul is longing to reach you like a burnt land that does not expect any sprouts from its ashes. Lord! Don't leave me alone in this desert. Send down the rain of your forgiveness on my barren soul and make my empty sky a bird. O Ghafar!

My eyes do not see any light except the window of your mercy.

I pull the backpack of hope on my tired pollen.

Divine! The cobwebs of sin have caught me so much that I have no hope of getting rid of ugliness and impurity; O my screamer! Your ugly servant who is tired of sin calls you.

God! Which furnace should I take refuge in?

What power should I use so that I don't taste your blessing!?

Is separation from you possible? (And it is not possible to escape from your government(

Divine! Hopefully, I am surprised by your grace that without your look, what can be done?

As a particle that explores the path to reach the sun and rises in line with this ultimate manifestation, we seek you.

The absolute end! How can I say no to you, when I breathe at your will?

How can I not mention your name, whose language borrows words from you?

How can I bow my head on the altar of your love when my existence is meant for worshiping you.

God! I submit myself to the light of your dignity and close my eyes of hope on every false claimant; I open my hands and abandon myself in your endless kingdom.

I remove from my body, the garment of sin, I remove the festering garment of doubt. I wear the ugly clothes of anxiety.

you read me Repeatedly; To your endless kindness, to your promises of punishment, to your abundance of kindness, to your successive tidings, to your occasional warnings.

you read me Repeatedly; to the shadows of your mercy, to the overcoming of your ability, to the abundance of your greatness, to the remaining foundations of your permanence;

you read me Repeatedly; To the eternity that you have spread in the world, to the eternity that you have called me to.

you read me Repeatedly; And I am still full of love for you, and I ask you for a respite for tomorrow; Maybe tomorrow!...

I read you Repeatedly; But the kindest! Forgive me if, with all your kindness, I have been hanged by the hands of sinners like this.

Forgive me if you have called me many times and I have not taken a step in response to your kindness, forgive me if I ask you again...!

The praise is special to you; that the treasures of your kindness are abundant.

I express your praise that you have shown us the straight path and made my creatures noble.

The splendor of your dignity is eternal; Help me to be worthy of this infinite grace of yours.

Oh pure purity! Mirror, purify my heart with the lights of your beautiful heart.

O all greatness and beauty! Make the long nights of my need like the morning of your answer and light.

cover my disgrace with your dignity; Or the star of defects!

I call you with your heavenly names! Or morning or holy!

I have been looking at your door for a long time.

You told me to call you to answer my prayer!

I read; More burning than every time, tearful and restless than every day.

Shine on me the rays of your mercy and build in my heart the palace of your presence so that I will be alive with your mention and we will fly in the air of your presence.

Bring this tiny drop to the sea of your mercy, fill these trembling hands with your mercy and bring this wandering wave to the shore of your mercy.

Gate of hope

Divine! I am imprisoned in the cage of my breath, I want a window to open my wings.

Help me to fulfill my promise and be your righteous servant.

Flow the breeze of your mercy in the plain of my need and read the height of my supplication from my longing gaze.

Kindly! Peace be upon Muhammad and his holy God.

Through the window of all the close and good people of your door, I look towards you with the eyes of hope.

Fill my needy hands with your mercy.

God!

How can I leave your door in despair when you are my support? Or Arham al-Rahimin.

O incomparable creator! Help me to walk through the dark paths of neglect.

Take my hand to free me from the chains of selfishness and rebellion.

help me To distance myself from the darkness of the soul and burn this tired soul to ashes in the flames of repentance.

God! The fragrance of your presence gives me renewed enthusiasm to cry out to you.

Your name grows a flower of hope and salvation in the desert of pain, and your remembrance heals wounded and painful hearts.

Fill the leaf of my thought with the buds of faith and decorate my actions with the jewel of sincerity.

Lord! I cling to the string of your mercy, forgive my mistakes and release your anger on me.

God! His peace is in your memory; I calm my restless soul with the voice of Lord.

Stop my heart from beating in the pulse of desires and make my longing soul fall in love with you.

The song of love

Divine! I am writing for you and in your name, who is a constant and ever-flowing presence of my moments and in these my tears are crystallized. Untie the shackles of the lessons of my will and the chains of daily life from the feet of my rebellion.

Divine! I did not learn how to praise you, how to love you; Teach me to be filled with you, help me not to be empty of myself.

May the weight of the road and the difficulty of my end, forgive the green leaf of my faith and make the blossoming of your love in my being, captive to the hands of the accident.

Take my life under the control of your love; The way you mixed my beginnings with your love.

God! Help me so that I don't think you're a stranger and earthly loves don't make me forget you, so that I can sing the song of your love and sing the ode of your love.

Help me so that the sea of my desires overflows and my heart does not become a bed of unreasonable desires.

Let me reach you with all the parts of my body and fill the volume of my being with your knowledge. And give me a respite, as you have always given me.

God! Help us to remove the roots of our beliefs from the clutches of termites.

May the fingers of accusation be pointed at me from all sides and my humanity be ruined!

God! look at me Your look revives life in me and makes me all mania.

You know the best name

In the name of God, whose blessing is the strength of bodies and whose mercy is the strength of souls!

Lives burn without ashes in his love and bitterness turns into sweetness effortlessly.

Other than him, one should go to the door and on his way to the head; That is not the way to go.

In the manifestation of his Moses-like beauty, one should become unconscious.

From the other side, all this loyalty and from this side, all this persecution!

Today, what did he do wrong in front of you, that you are turning him back so much, you will not be afraid of tomorrow, and if it is, then it is today. So when are you tomorrow?

Do you know who you are fighting? If children run away from home, they don't run and look after their mother at dinner time.

Dinner is coming and darkness is approaching, get up and sing!

Stand up as he himself said: read me so that I will answer you!

Who is a friend who doesn't take heart from Atabi and doesn't go?

And who is a friend who doesn't go his own way and join another?

0 lasting

I feel that all the alleys of the earth are hollowed out under the steps of desperate passers-by. The sun is the memory of the distant years of the sky, and the sky is the memory of the distant years of the earth.

I feel like I have lost someone around my childhood. A wonderful strangeness pours out from my fingers. I hang from my eyes and cry; Like a dervish without a belt or an axe, in a cold monastery, tired of the earth and longing for the sky.

I run and stop. I look behind me; Nothing! ... Ahead, nothing! A huge whirlwind twists my silence. I want to scream, but it's like, the voice becomes a stone in my throat and there is silence again.

God! My soul is a volcano of pain; I erupt and collapse. I burn and burn. My world is dark and windowless. My life is a repetition of springless years, icy years.

Post boxes return my letters.

The birds don't want my sky. Children do not return my smiles. Where did I come from that even the trees withhold their shadows from me?

God! These alleys smell of not coming, the smell of going and not arriving.

The taste of the long nights of these moments is of sunset and homelessness.

my God! You are the reason I am great; The reason for my crying and smiling is my pride in living.

I am destitute and helpless, I am helpless and without support; I have come for you to hold my hand and listen to me.

Accept me and be my support.

I want to be the neighbor of the sun and always the sky; Find me and accept my plea, (O Most Merciful(

God! I am alone and helpless, I miss a fresh air, I miss you.

I am tired of all this wandering, of all this doubt, of going and not arriving; It is as if all the doors of the world are closed to me.

God! I am too strange that anyone but you can be the salve of my old homelessness.

Like the fishes separated from the sea, lying on the beach sand and gasping for air, I gasp for air and cannot find a way out.

Sometimes I think that I am so far from you and insignificant in your opinion, that no matter how I run your roads, I will not reach the gate of your fame.

Lord! I am a lost traveler, naked and without luggage, I did not endure your sky and the earth will not endure me either.

The earth is a big prison, full of chains and locks, and I am my jailer. Who but you can remove the locks from my hands and mouth and set me free?

God! I hear you in the hooting of wild horses, when their hooves shake the heart of the plain. I see you in the innocent eyes of a girl who sells apples, when her little hands smell of begging.

You are; I am the one who has closed my sinful eyes to the world of your kindness and left your loving arms.

God! Forgive me if I was careless. If I were blind and didn't see you. If I was far away and did not hear you; that you are forgiving, covering mistakes and accepting repentance.

God!

The flames of sin have burned the land of my existence. The wind blows and scatters my ashes. The wind blows and every piece of me is thrown aside. I hide behind my cloudy look so that I don't see the last particles of my ashes. I don't believe that I have been crushed under my step!

I embrace my longings and say; Who but you can make the burnt trees of my existence bloom?

I have forgotten my hazy memories with the hope of the sun of your grace.

Divine!

In the most stormy moments of my life, it is the flickering light of your mercy that lights my way and guides the broken boat of my heart to the shore of salvation.

God of rainy skies!

O hope of worried hearts, O good and kind! These eyes, tired of the darkness, are constantly searching for your light, these feverish feet have been walking these rough roads for years hoping to reach you;

Help me to serve you as you deserve; as you want O eternal immortal!

The sound of broken grudges

When the heavy burden of sin burns the back of my faith.

When the termites of doubt fall on my faith and the volume of my loneliness is more than I can bear, you hear the sound of my broken grudges from the depth of silence and fill my troubled solitude with light.

My heart has made a home behind the gates of sin.

The unruly horse of my soul is unbridled, going forward to destruction forever.

The hands of the rebels have been exposed from the stain of my pride and ignorance and they are giving life to the fire of torment.

I miss the darkness of sin. I want to tell you the story of my sorrows in the bright shade of grace and forgiveness and empty the heavy burden of my eyes on seal and prayer, hope and forgiveness.

These nights, the request of my prayers, is your pure look, on the loneliness of a girl who swallows her body and sheds her tears in the hiding place of the night. The seeds of my rosary whisper the remembrance of your kindness, and the ever-open Mufatih stretches out its hands of need and begging towards the province of answer.

This peace is the interpretation of the truth that overflows from your words; The truth that polishes the soul.

The truth that promises a bright tomorrow; Tomorrow, in the color of answer, in the color of trust...

Tonight, all my words are cloaked in poetry and wisdom.

I have opened my heart to you as it is. I am sitting on the simplicity of this table and I spend all my moments in prayer until dawn.

I hope for your clear answer. I believe in your truth and I am sure of the truthfulness of your answer.

Don't take me for my rebellion! Look at the sincerity of my words! Don't disappoint my hopeful prayers!

You are my peace

Divine! In the solitude of my homelessness, I remember you that you will remember my presence.

If you don't want, there won't be the smallest sign of me on earth, and if you want, I will reach the highest peak of presence, which is to reach you.

Divine!

The prosperity of my empty moments is the mention of your memory, which itself is an endless capital.

Whoever thinks of living forever will find immortality in you.

Divine!

Broken hearts are the interpretation of nightly cries that are calmed by your memory (only with the remembrance of Allah, Tatimin al-Qulob.(

Divine!

Whoever shines a particle of your light in his being, he has insured the inner sun (straight path) forever.

Divine!

You have planted seeds of certainty on the side of our street of doubt, from which green plants of faith will blossom.

Divine!

In the tiling of the altar of my gaze, flowers of faith are imprinted, which are tied to your Kaaba.

Divine!

Drop by drop, my secrets and needs are a clear river that flows towards you.

Divine!

Your place of worship is a green garden whose four seasons are always spring, and white agave flowers grow on its towering pulpit, the smell of which has made the angels swoon.

Divine!

You have made the moon mad, the stars have chained it, and you have created the sun free to shine.

Divine!

If the sea is the sea, it is your desire and if the desert is the desert, it is your desire.

You have pulled the threads of our hearts into the lights of your mystical nights.

Divine!

We have opened a carpet the size of a plain, facing the Qibla of your sky, so that the royal bird of our hearts will fly towards its mirror.

And we have connected the dirt road of our empire with a bridge of love to the boundless sea of certainty, so that we can climb on its waves.

Divine!

We have weighed the world and you with the heaviest weight of truth on both sides of the scales of conscience and we have found that the truth is you.

Divine!

If the sky of our deeds is covered by a black cloud of sin, we clear it with rain (repentance); Because you are kind and merciful.

Divine!

We are close to you and we are separated from everyone and we are sitting at the door of your prayer; In the hope that you will not leave us alone for a moment.

Divine!

O Lord of the worlds, O God of night and day, O answerer of desperate cries! What I said and you heard, all my loving prayers were directed to you. So find me, I won't get home without you!

Barrels! I subjected my conscience, which you have breathed into it from your soul and made it brighter than the rain and clearer than the sound of canaries and the dance of the shaparkas on the shoulders of the breeze, I subjected to the poisonous winds of sin!

I plunged my soul into the darkest and deepest moments of rebellion and attached my heart to long and distant desires!

With every breath that I took out of the tightness of my chest, I was one step further from you and one step closer to death, and I was still wandering in a sleep of neglect and ignorance; A dream that was infected with nightmares and painful moments of neglect, loneliness and destitution of my soul.

I counted my sins as small, and in that state, I found myself pleased, and you saw all this while with only a corner of your eternal and infinite power, you could crush me with all my low desires and great sins. .

God! It was you who kept me in the shelter of your grace and care from the days of darkness and fearlessness and the curtain of the doors of my soul until the moments of repentance and shame of my sins, and at that time when I deserved to be burned, the fire of your anger was on my soul. You did not make my rebelliousness aflame and you sheltered me to enter the valley of your love and affection.

God! You brought me from the depth of destruction to the height of light; you helped me While I didn't deserve it, and with the light of faith, you gave my soul peace that achieving none of my dreams would give me.

God! I heard your kind voice through the verses of your guidance.

Yes! I heard your voice calling me to the lights and lighting up the stars of faith in the sky of my heart.

God! I have brought me to your door with a heart full of hope, save me from my self-destruction and in the vagaries of negligence and sin, and make me benefit from the wind of your care!

I want you...

I return to you, O God, who poured the wine of love into the cup of my heart and filled me with passion to be with you, you took my hands when I was stuck in this mortal land.

Now give me a balm to my broken wings so that I can fly to the peak of flight; To show the sky that although I am earthly, I am more heavenly than all my birds.

Just draw a red line on my sins and mistakes and register my name in the book of names of your worthy servants.

I ask you for help; You know all the needs of my heart. I ask you for help; You are the first and last hope of my longing nights and you know how close

I get to the devil when I am away from you and how unnecessarily I spend my days and nights.

I ask you for help; Because of you, my being is filled with intoxication and all the sorrows of the world fill my heart.

take my hands The warmth of your hands calms the anxiety of my heart and leads me to the light.

My restless soul is more thirsty than it can be satisfied with these sips of love. My soul wants the sea of your love and the ocean of your knowledge.

I ask you to remove me from the passion of temptations, continuous and endless pride and longing for the world.

I ask you to give me the strength to fight against the army of demons and pour an iron will in me so that I can reach the farthest heaven of your worship.

Be my support

I have relied on a support that I don't have. I am attached to the door that is closed and I am oblivious to you; From you, my only creator! Ah, when I was drunk and euphoric, I did not see anyone but myself, and now, helpless and distraught, I have brought the burden of pain to Karim's door.

Divine! I envy those who are blessed with the blessing of gratitude; They too, who were not neglected by the glittering windows of the world, and whatever they saw of the artefacts, they remembered Sane.

Divine! Leave the ashes of this half-burnt body like a flameless candle to the breeze of your forgiveness; Maybe he extinguished the flame of selfishness and neglect of you!

Which blessing should I open my mouth to be thankful for, and which blessing should I look forward to and know that I did not neglect others!?

I shout; In harmony with the burnt sounds of your lovers; Those who have seen you many times and heard your voice in the flowing rivers, those who saw nothing but you, and whatever they heard, heard nothing but your voice.

Divine! Like a ecstatic butterfly, I have surrendered my free will to the light of your love and I have submitted myself to your will so that you can burn me with the fire of your love and polish this tired existence with the light of your love.

Divine! I wish I could say that I have been nothing except what you asked and I have done nothing except what you said! Hey! I have entrusted my freedom to the nameless hands of my tempting self.

Divine! From which window, the extent of your presence can't be seen and in which window you can't sit and watch? From which larynx can we not hear your voice and with which sight can we not see you!?

How futile is running away? You can never escape from yourself.

How useless it is to find a helper other than you and how pitiful it is to seek a mother other than you!

God! I turn away from looking at the silent world around me to explore inside; The inside that should be the temple of your remembrance and be caressed by the light of your mercy; But it is the fire of being away from you that turns my existence into black ash and unhappiness.

O Fiyaz! Which way should I look without a sign of you and which light should I sit and watch without emanating from you!?

God! The pen in the path of describing you, like a stupid foot, stuck on the road of Wasal, is surprised by your greatness. Which word should I choose that can express your glory?

Divine! I am afraid of which burnt song and which dawnless dinner; When I have you and I have relied on the pillar of your favors and I have raised the hand of trust in your province?

Divine! The hyenas of doubt bite my faith and separate me from the door of your Lordship. God! Petitioner and supplicant, I present my glories to you and I humbly request that you remove from me the excuses of staying away from your holy province so that I may be worthy to enter.

Divine! I have relied on the support that I don't have and I have attached my heart to the door that is closed; You are the light of the windows in front of me and you are the support of my loneliness...

Endless ocean

Star in the eye

Night backpack on the back

I kneel before you.

I have not come from a long way; that (you are closer to me than the jugular vein(

I am dark

So much so that I hang on the tiny light of the firefly.

Or light!

Enlighten me from your eternal light!

With a lightning that burns the threshing floor of my black work!

Give me a light that looks at darkness!

I am tired;

I am looking for another sky;

The bottom of the ocean is a different color.

I am restless;

Like willow hairs falling on the shoulders of the wind.

My eyes are a river that has overflowed and my hands are a dove that longs for the sky.

O companion of restless hearts, O peace of turbulent hearts!

Fill me with a calmness that will not fall with any storm.

O Lord!

Only the whisper of your memory calms me down.

reference

-Meshkini, Ali, Holy Quran

-Abolhassan Hossein bin Muhammad, Seyyed Razi; Translation: Shirvani, Ali, Nahj al-Balagheh, first edition, Qom, Dar al-Alam publishing house, 1383 AH.

-Kahami, Ali, 2009, Recognizing asceticism in the Holy Quran, Research Quarterly Journal of Ethics Research, 49 (181-203)

-Amini, Ebrahim, 1372, Islam and Education, Tehran, Association of Parents and Teachers.

-Ashrafi, Amir; Hosseini Sarasht, Seyyed Mohammad Sadiq, the works of piety in this world and the hereafter inspired by the verses of the Qur'an and the words of the Ahl al-Bayt (peace be upon him), Ethic Magazine, 16(5-68)

-Tamimi Amadi, Abdul Waheed (1366), Gharral al-Hakem and Derral al-Hakem, Qom, Islamic Propaganda Office.

-Jabaran, Mohammad Reza, 2013, conceptual analysis of lifestyle, Qobsat magazine, issue 10 of the 20th year.

-Mohammadi Ray Shahri, Muhammad, Encyclopaedia of Amir al-Mominin (peace be upon him), translation: Mehrizi, Mahdi, vol. 4.

-Shariati, Ali, Shahadat, Tehran, Bina Publications.

-Sabouri Kazaj, Parviz, Javad, 2019, the study of an ideal society in the lives of the martyrs of the holy defense, two quarterly scientific research journals of the Cultural Guard of the Islamic Revolution, Faculty of Islamic Humanities and Soft Power University of Officer Training and Guards of Imam Hossein (peace be upon him), 22(10)) (179-181)

-Tabarsi, Fazl bin Hassan (1389). Makarem al-Akhlaq, Qom: Naghma Qur'an Publications.

-Kaviani, Mohammad (2011). Islamic life style. Qom: University and District Research Institute.

-Motahari, Morteza (1367). Education in Islam, Sadra, Tehran.

-Motahari, Morteza, Teacher's Notes, Tehran, Sadra Publications, 2013.

-Teacher of ethics, printing and publishing center of the field of representation of religious jurist in Sepah

-The article on the educational works of Taqwa, Hosni, Shaban Ali.

-Let's review the article of sincerity. Author: Javad Khorrami.

-Maleki, Hamid; Nobakht, Mohammad, 2019, The lifestyle of a spiritual person from the perspective of Islam, Journal of Research in Islamic Education and Training, 49(21), (181-203)

-Moinipour, Massoud; Lakzaei, Reza; Zarifian, Mohammad Hossein, Explanation of the religious lifestyle based on sermon 193 of Nahj al-Balaghe, Ethical research paper, 27(8), (103-124.(

-Hashemi Ardakani, Seyyed Hassan, 2018, Educational factors in the path of human perfection from the perspective of Nahj al-Balaghah, Islamic Education Quarterly, Number 8, Year 4.

- Yadalhi Far, Mohammad Javad Faqihi, 2017, the goals and principles of spiritual inheritance based on the teachings of Imam Ali (peace be upon him), Nahj al-Balagheh Research Quarterly, number 24, sixth year.

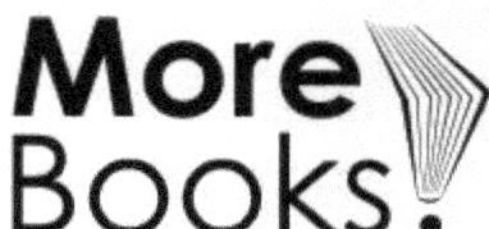
More
Books!

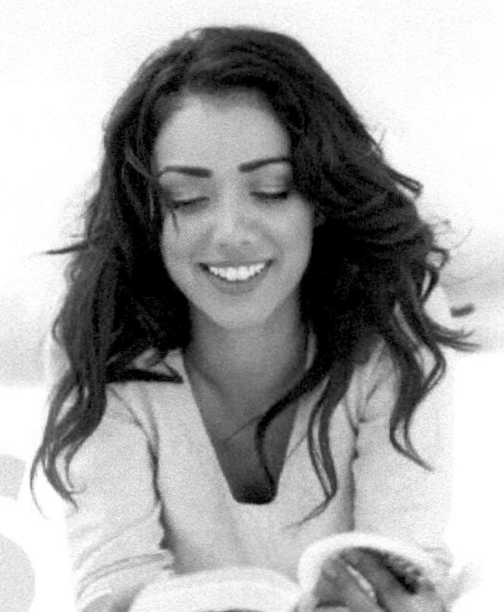

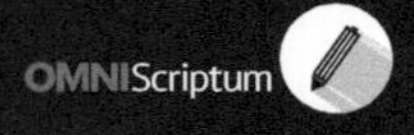
OMNIScriptum

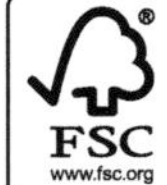

Printed by Books on Demand GmbH, Norderstedt / Germany